REINHARD

C000053199

THE
LORD, YOUR
HEALER

HIS DIVINE 'MEDICAL INSURANCE' PLAN

Australia • Brazil • Canada • Czech Republic • Germany • Hong Kong • Kenya • Latin America
• New Zealand • Nigeria • Singapore • South Africa • United Kingdom • United States

THE LORD YOUR HEALER

©2022 Harvester Services – Reinhard Bonnke

Published by Christ for all Nations
PO Box 590588 Orlando, FL 32859-0588
www.CfaN.org

ISBN 978-3-935057-14-1

Editor Kimberly Overcast
Layout Oleksandr M Volyk

Printed in Colombia

THE LORD, YOUR HEALER

The why and how of divine healing

GOD'S NATIONAL HEALTH SCHEME

Jesus Christ is the *Great Physician* on call day and night. His surgery never closes, and we don't have to wait for an appointment. He specializes in all kinds of troubles, whether sickness of the soul, afflictions of the body, or the ills of society. There are no fees.

We all enjoy good health—when we have it! Unfortunately, so many people get up in the morning feeling run down, and start the day already exhausted, which was never God's idea. The Gospel of Jesus Christ is the national health scheme for every nation on earth, and the Bible is its textbook. Somebody said that God meant our bodies to last, with care, a lifetime!

The first page of the Bible says, "God saw everything that He had made, and indeed it was very good" (Genesis 1:31). The last page says, "There shall be no more death, nor sorrow, nor crying ... no more pain" (Revelation 21:4). Things began very well, and they will end that way.

Sickness in God's good world is like weeds growing among wheat. But make no mistake—God did not sow the weeds. "An enemy did this" (Matthew 13:28, NIV). God sent Jesus who "went about...healing all who were oppressed by the devil, for God was with Him" (Acts 10:38). It was the Creator's protest against the sabotage of His work by the devil.

God planted cures in nature that medical research keeps finding. But the God who heals naturally also heals supernaturally. Scripture denies that sickness is God's will, and it credits healings to God. Today His hand touches far more people than many realize. Throughout the world, many supernatural healings take place every year, proving that "Jesus Christ is the same yesterday, today, and forever" (Hebrews 13:8). In our own CfaN crusades, outstanding wonders regularly take place.

PART ONE

WHY WE CAN BE HEALED

1. We can expect healing because Jesus never changes.

Jesus healed multitudes. That was His mission. He came to heal as well as to save. He did not come from glory to earth for only those people who happened to be alive during that period in history. He did not come to bring relief merely to a few thousand people. That was only the beginning. The Bible says it was what "Jesus...*began* to do" (Acts 1:1, emphasis added). By His deeds, He showed us what He wanted to do, so that we can see what He was—and still is—like. He came to heal *them* so that He could heal *you* and *me*.

People living in the days of Jesus' earthly ministry possibly thought of Jesus more as a Healer than anything else. He set out to heal. That was Jesus. He didn't wait for the sick to come to Him—He often went to them. The Apostle Peter actually said that Jesus went around for that very purpose (Acts 10:38). Healing was a major part of His mission, and Jesus said God sent Him to do those very works (John 5:17; 9:3–4).

THE PEAK OF HIS POWER

We read, "Jesus Christ is the same yesterday, today, and forever" (Hebrews 13:8). Jesus is alive, just as ready to heal now as He ever was. He is not like the moon which has phases, sometimes showing a darkened portion. He is Sun of Righteousness, risen with healing in His wings (Malachi 4:2).

What Jesus was, He is—constantly and forever. Miracles are part and parcel of the Gospel of Jesus Christ, not something added on as an afterthought. From start to finish Christianity is supernatural, beginning as resurrection life and power. Healings demonstrate the essential truths of Christianity and show us Jesus as He really is.

Look at James 1:17:

> *Every good gift and every perfect gift is from above,*
> *and comes down from the Father of lights, with whom*
> *there is no variation or shadow of turning.*

James has a picture of a sundial in mind. The sun rises and sets. As we see it move across the sky, the shadow moves across the sundial. Then comes a moment when there is no shadow. At midday the sun reaches its zenith, or meridian, and the shadow disappears. After noon it begins to decline, and the shadow creeps slowly across the dial. That is what the ordinary sun does.

In contrast to the sun, James considers the "Father of lights." Jesus Christ is the Light of all lights, the Light of the world, and there is no changing with Him causing a shadow. He is always at the peak of His power, forever at the zenith. "There is no variation or shadow of turning." He never turns, never inclines or declines, never rises or sets. He is always at the height of His glory, pouring out His

6

love and life in all His fullness and brilliance. That is why millions are being healed today.

If we look back, we see that what Jesus was then, He is now. If we look forward, we see that He will be what He was. He is not *becoming* great; He is great. He is now at the height of His greatness. He always was—and will always be—the Healer and the Saviour.

THE YESTERDAY, TODAY, FOREVER CHRIST

Here is an example from Luke's Gospel (7:11–16). Jesus raised a young man, the son of a widow, from the dead in the village of Nain. We read that Jesus had compassion on the weeping mother. In the same region the great prophets Elijah and Elisha had both also raised mothers sons from the dead (1 Kings 17; 2 Kings 4). That was eight hundred years before.

Now notice this. In each case, the Bible says Elijah and Elisha gave the son back to his mother and *Jesus did exactly the same.* He raised the young man from death and gave him back to his mother. Christ knew the Scriptures, and it was His pointed way of showing that what He had just done for this grieving mother, He had done long before for other mothers. It was He who had raised those two sons from death. Jesus had been around in Israel long before His birth in Bethlehem and had worked through Elijah and Elisha. Eight centuries made no difference to His power or compassion. Generation after generation has experienced Christ's healing touch. We recognize His fingerprints, His typical way of working. He is like the noonday sun and never switches off. His powerful sunlight kills the virus of evil.

7

2. We can expect healing because God started it.

Healing originated with God. It wasn't our idea. At the beginning of the Bible, when nobody had ever thought of such a thing, He healed people. That was four thousand years ago. "So Abraham prayed to God; and God healed Abimelech, his wife, and his female servants" (Genesis 20:17). Nobody suggested healing to God or begged Him for it. He did it because it was His nature. He loved to do it.

If there is something you don't like doing, you keep quiet about it. If you enjoy doing something—perhaps a hobby or a sport—you devote time to it and generally talk about it, too. God didn't keep quiet about healing—He couldn't! His heart was full of compassion. He not only talked about it, but *did* it as well.

When Jesus came, He offered to heal people. We read in John's Gospel that He performed some of His miracles without being specifically asked. He went to the Pool of Bethesda, where there were hundreds of afflicted people, without anybody suggesting it. He approached one paralyzed man and asked him if he wished to be healed. The man didn't even say yes, but Jesus healed him anyway (John 5). Later, He saw a blind man and without even asking him what he wanted, Jesus restored his sight (John 9). That's Jesus. That was Jesus yesterday, and that is Jesus today.

If a man spends eight years or more studying to become a doctor, when he has finished his studies, he will open a practice to treat sick people. It would be ridiculous for a doctor not to practice after all his efforts to qualify. We read

8

in Matthew 8:17: "He Himself took our infirmities and bore our sicknesses." That is a quotation from Isaiah 53, about the crucifixion. Christ bore our pains and our sins in His own body on the Cross. If Jesus died for us, it is not too much to expect Him to heal us.

3. We can expect healing because of God's name.

God's name is *Yahweh Rapha,* "The Lord who heals you." That is like His badge of office as the Great Healer. It was given when Moses was leading Israel out of slavery. After three days passing through a waterless wasteland, they were desperate. Then they arrived at the pool of Marah, only to find the water bitter, undrinkable. The people were angry with Moses. There was only one thing that Moses knew he could do—cry out to God. And God performed a special wonder. He healed the bitter waters of Marah to demonstrate who He was—the Lord who heals (Exodus 15:22–26).

The great span of God's goodness began to be apparent. The God who healed Marah's bitter waters would heal the foul waters of the whole world, cleansing it of bitterness. He gave us His name, *Yahweh Rapha,* "I am the Lord who heals you." Nobody now has to draw his own conclusions about His identity. His name tells us who He is. He heals, and in His glory He is doing just that. Healing is the music of His soul.

"The Lord who heals" was His name not exclusively for Israel, but for everybody. What God is in one place, He must always be everywhere "God is the King of all the earth" (Psalm 47:7). Just as I am myself in Germany or Britain, and you are you in one place or another, so the Lord is the same all over the world. God is God everywhere. There is not one kind of God in Israel and another in Europe or Africa. Every year, He is the same God; He does not change with the seasons or the passing of the years. "I am who I am....I am the Lord who heals you.... I do not change" (Exodus 3:14;15:26, Malachi 3:6). In fact, everything that God is, He always is. Everywhere, all the time, He is holy, righteous, merciful, a shepherd, the Savior, and also the Healer.

4. We can expect healing because it is in God's character to put right what is wrong.

That is what the whole Bible is about—wrongs being righted. That includes the wrong of suffering. Scripture begins with the Book of Genesis, describing the greatest of all miracles— creation. The earth was formless, dark, and empty. Then God turned it into the beautiful globe we now know. Likewise today, the Spirit of the Lord moves to transform whatever else He sees that is dark and disturbed. The desert blossoms as the rose, the rubble of bombed cities blooms with wild flowers, sinners become saints, the sick are made whole.

When evil entered, the garden of Eden withered. Then the Lord stepped in with His plan of redemption. He continues to work out His plan to this very day. "My Father has been working until now, and I have been working," said Jesus (John 5:17). Romans chapter 8 promises that the whole creation will be delivered from corruption. The last book in the Bible tells us that the leaves of the tree of life will be used for "the healing of the nations" (Revelation 22:2). Healing by leaves! God does not work by brute force but by mercy. We can come to God confident of His sympathy in our physical need. Our self-curing mechanism has been broken. People are ill and God is unhappy about it.

5. We can expect healing because God's mercies are for everybody.

After Jesus had been away from Narazeth for about a year, He went back and preached in the synagogue that He had once so faithfully attended (Luke 4:16–30). In His sermon, He talked about Naaman. This man was a leper, a foreign army general from Syria who had taken some Israelite people captive. He had an Israelite slave girl. But God still healed him (2 Kings 5). Jesus also talked about a widow, similarly a foreigner. God sent Elijah to her and, during a famine, fed not only the widow and Elijah but the widow's family as well. Jesus was showing that God was concerned with people everywhere, not just the chosen people.

In fact, the first people to experience divine healing were Philistines. God sent them to Abraham, who would pray for them and they would be healed (Genesis 20). Abraham certainly did not trust them, and later the Philistines became Israel's enemies. But God's mercies are worldwide. He doesn't heal great saints only, but sinful people as well.

6. We can expect healing because of God's promises.

It would need a book, not a booklet, to quote all the promises of God, but one quotation which is typical can be found in James 5:14-15: "The prayer of faith will save the sick, and the Lord will raise him up. And if he has committed sins, he will be forgiven."

Actually, every time Christ healed someone, it was also a promise. Whatever God did, He did it to show us what He *will* do. The works of Jesus are prophecies and signs. To heal just a few sick individuals in the past was never His plan or wish. Some people have suggested it was, but nothing they ever wrote is utterly convincing. We cannot believe that of Jesus. His earthly ministry was a *demonstration of what He is. It was meant to encourage our faith.* Healing was a major part of Christ's ministry. We cannot write it off as having no connection with our present needs. People get sick now just as they did then. Jesus knows that this is the case, which is why we have the Gospels to tell us what He did about it. It is all there, full of significance, for our hope and comfort. It can mean only one thing—Jesus still heals today!

Some people have the upside-down idea that giving testimonies about healing is wrong in case it builds up false hopes in others. This is really a criticism of the Gospels, which are full of such testimonies. The stories are bound to create faith. They are surely there to do so. If you don't want to encourage people to look for healing, don't let them see the Bible! No book generates such a wealth of hope as the Bible. No preacher encouraged people like Jesus. Every Scripture testimony is like God saying, "Try me now in this" (Malachi 3:10).

7. We can expect healing because Jesus said "I will".

To create trust in God, the Bible gives us story after story. The New Testament turns the spotlight first on a leper (Matthew 8:1–3). Jesus had just come down after giving His Sermon on the Mount, and this victim of disease met Him. He said, "If you are *willing,* You *can* make me clean." That is the crucial question for many people. *Will* God do what He can?

First, we all need to know that He *can.* God is the Almighty. If He could not heal the sick, He would not be Almighty, and thus not God. In Jeremiah 32:27 we read God's question: "Behold, I am the LORD, the God of all flesh. Is there anything too hard for me?" No answer was needed. God calls Himself the "God of all flesh." God can heal flesh.

So He *can,* but *will* He? The story in Matthew 8 gives us the answer. "Jesus put out His hand and touched him, saying, 'I am willing; be cleansed.' Immediately his leprosy was cleansed." Immediately afterwards, we see in the same chapter a Roman centurion who had a servant who was ill. Jesus said, "I *will* come and heal him" (v. 7, emphasis added). Those two words I will reveal God's heart. Christ's words never pass away. His "I will" is a cosmic law. His words are written in heaven, carved in the foundation of the world. It is God's "Amen!" to our hopes, written into the constitution of the Kingdom of God.

God says, "I will," countless times throughout the Old Testament. The words are the key to God's covenanted promises to bless the world. The first covenant (Genesis 9)

shows God wanting to take care of every creature on earth—
it is one big I will from start to finish. Exodus is a book
of God's covenant with Israel and I will is used nearly one
hundred times. It comes forty-six times in just six chapters of
Isaiah, and nineteen times in one chapter of Jeremiah (chapter
31). When Jesus said, "I will," it gathered all God's hundreds
of I will promises and focused their power like a laser beam
on the leper, burning out his disease. God's I will includes
His will to heal.

In the matter of healing, God still says, "I will." Somebody
might say, "I was prayed for and not healed, so it is not God's
will." The logic is wrong. There could be other reasons. Not
being healed has nothing to do with the will of God. God
doesn't change His mind—not just for you! You may not
be healed, although *it is certainly His will.* God's will is not
always done, which is why Christ taught us to pray, "Your
will be done." He said that "men always ought to pray and
not lose heart" (Luke 18:1). Many sail in such shallow waters
of faith, their keel grinds on the gravel all the way to glory!

8. *We can expect healing because Christ introduced the Kingdom of God into this world.*

The Kingdom of God is a kind of fourth dimension, a
supernatural order with power to override the natural order.
The hand of a man can make things happen that would
normally not happen naturally, and so can the hand of God.
Jesus brought the powers of heaven to people on earth.
Christianity is miraculous.

9. *We can expect healing for the greatest reason of all:*

Christ died for us. Here are two wonderful Bible encouragements: "He who did not spare His own Son, but delivered Him up for us all, how shall He not with Him also freely give us all things?" (Romans 8:32). "He Himself took our infirmities and bore our sicknesses" (Matthew 8:17). The Lord made heaven and earth. Jesus conquered death. He does not give up at the sight of a mere cripple or a cancer.

PART TWO

HOW WE CAN BE HEALED

We can be healed by the laying on of hands.

This is the normal Scriptural pattern. Jesus said of those who follow Him, "They will lay hands on the sick, and they will recover" (Mark 16:18). The ordinary hands of an ordinary person bring about a miraculous change in an afflicted person. How? It is quite simple—that is the way God planned it. Mortals become retailers of His wholesale blessings. Divine power operates through manpower. That is a great principle. It runs through all creation. It seems futile to bury a seed for it to die, but God brings it to life to spring up and bear fruit. It may seem futile to put our hands on a person, but that is nonetheless all God wants. It produces wonders. We plant; God gives the increase. We lay on hands: He heals.

We preach; He saves. Why did God plan it like that? First, God wants us to be channels of His love. He sheds His love in our hearts for us to carry it to others in a practical way. People see that God loves them, and it teaches us to serve others with love. Second, God wants to share His pleasure with us. He takes delight in blessing and healing and saving. If we work with Him, we share that delight. He says, "Enter into the joy of your Lord" (Matthew 25:23).

We can be healedbby praying when afflicted.

Divine healing is a branch of the subject of prayer. Many thousands of people have recovered as they prayed. God always hears your prayers. Sometimes God does not give you a direct and personal reply, but sends the answer through a human channel such as the ministry of one of His servants. The "gifts of healings" (1 Corinthians 12:9) are for that purpose. God gives healings to somebody to steward. That person is responsible for bringing healing to sick people who have prayed. You pray; God sends the answer through them.

Often I have known that I had a healing for someone who had been praying, and they have come forward in the service and received it. In one meeting in Norway God kept saying "paralysis" to me until I prayed for the person, unknown to me, who was suffering from this affliction. A woman at the back of the crowd had often sought God on that very matter, and that day He sent the answer. I was a bit like a dispatch rider from God. So all over the world, the vast majority of people find deliverance through the ordinance of laying on of hands, sometimes accompanied by anointing with oil (Mark 16:18; James 5:14–16). Obedience to the Word of God brings blessing.

We can be healed without doing anything about it ourselves.

A woman was carried into one of our campaign meetings in a coma, and by the Holy Spirit I became aware of it. When I declared that God had whispered this information to me, He immediately touched her and she became conscious and well. God touches children and babies, who can't understand. He heals people too ill to think. They can't do anything themselves, but they recover, simply by a sovereign act of God.

It is common for people to be healed without expecting it. In one of our Gospel campaigns, a gang came along to cause a riot. They brought a blind man as an excuse to stir up trouble if my prayers did not heal him. While he was just standing with them, his sight was restored. On another occasion a demented man came to a meeting and stood at the back of the crowd. Suddenly the Lord went across to him, without my doing anything. The evil spirit left him, and the man came to himself all at once and wondered what he was doing there! Sometimes God cannot wait for us to act. He is there to heal, and He does what He is there to do—He heals.

We can be healed through other people's faith.

James 5:14–16: "Is anyone among you sick? Let him call for the elders of the church, and let them pray over him....And the prayer of faith will save the sick, and the Lord will raise him up....pray for one another, that you may be healed."

In Mark 2:1–12, a man was brought to Jesus on a stretcher carried by four others. We read: "When Jesus saw *their* faith, he said to the paralyzed man... 'I tell you, get up, take your mat and go home.' He...walked out in full view of them all"[1] (NIV, emphasis added).

Prayers in our services have brought deliverance to people miles away who did not know they were being prayed for. Indeed, don't we all pray for absent friends—successfully? Doctors talk about "spontaneous" remissions. Nothing is spontaneous; there is always a cause. The world-famous poet

1 Alfred, Lord Tennyson, "Idylls of the King," University of Rochester, accessed February 22, 2022

18

Tennyson wrote, "More things are wrought by prayer than this world dreams of." He was right.

We can be healed through our own faith.

This brings us to what many see as a crucial matter. Little is said about faith in this booklet because so many give up at its very mention, as if faith was too much to ask of them. Take special note—*God does not do the impossible only by impossible faith.* He only wants possible faith—faith that is possible for you.

The disciples asked Jesus to increase their faith. From the millions of sermons preached you would think He would do just that, but He did not! He explained that faith is not a matter of size." If you have faith as a mustard seed, you can say to this mulberry tree,'Be pulled up by the roots and be planted in the sea,' and it would obey you" (Luke 17:5–6). Yet nobody has ever done it! In these days of technology, He would perhaps use a different image to illustrate his point and say, "If you have faith as a thin fuse wire, the full mains voltage of God can come to you." By the way, unbelief blows the fuse, not God's voltage.

Here are five facts about faith:

- Faith is your spiritual hand simply accepting what is offered.
- Faith is not a possession. It is decision, action, believing.
- Faith is greatest when you are least aware of it, when you act like a trusting child.
- Faith is letting God pick you up and carry you like a trusting child.
- Faith is leaving things to God.

If you feel you lack faith, don't worry; you can get faith for "faith comes by hearing, and hearing by the word of God" (Romans 10:17). The "why" part of this booklet brings you the Word of God. Read it again and again, then go and hear it preached. Check your "fuse"! Cast your doubts away, repent of unbelief, change your mind, and ask for the laying-on of hands.

THE BONUS

One final word: if you want healing only, you will miss a lot. Healing was made possible by the Cross, but Christ died to do much more than doctors. He died to bring us the far greater blessing of salvation, the forgiveness of sins and peace with God. He is not only a Healer but a Savior. Jesus said it was better to enter into life maimed than into hell fire whole (Matthew 18:8, Mark 9:43).

To accept healing but reject Christ is disastrous. In fact, millions of people are never healed because they reject the Healer. He doesn't *send* healing. He *brings* it Himself.

20

It is better to be saved than healed. Even better still is to have both: to receive Christ Himself, the Savior and Healer. "How shall He not with Him also freely give us all things?" (Romans 8:32).

Notes

BONNKE.TV

Welcome to **BONNKE.TV** – the digital home of Reinhard Bonnke sermons, tv shows, and films.

From classic messages to the latest live streams, this is your one-stop, 24/7 outlet for Evangelist Bonnke's passionate, insightful, Spirit-led preaching and teaching.

And, of course, feel free to share this site with your friends, family... anyone you think will be blessed by Reinhard Bonnke's singular voice and mountain-moving faith.

BONNKE
CLASSIC

CFAN
TV SHO

LEGAC

GODS
CALL

Evange
REINHARD B

RENEW YOUR FAITH

STREAMI
24/7

BE ENCOURAGED